Practical
Pre-School

Planning for Learning through

Growth

by Judith Harries
Illustrated by Cathy Hughes

Contents

Published by Step Forward Publishing Limited
The Coach House, Cross Road, Milverton, Leamington Spa, CV32 5PB Tel: 01926 420046
© Step Forward Publishing Limited 2002
Planning for Learning through Growth   ISBN: 1-902438-73-6

Making plans

WHY PLAN?

The purpose of planning is to make sure that all children enjoy a broad and balanced curriculum. All planning should be useful. Plans are working documents that you spend time preparing, but which should later repay your efforts. Try to be concise. This will help you in finding information quickly when you need it.

LONG-TERM PLANS

Preparing a long-term plan, which maps out the curriculum during a year or even two, will help you to ensure that you are providing a variety of activities and are meeting the statutory requirements of the *Curriculum Guidance for the Foundation Stage* (2000).

Your long-term plan need not be detailed. Divide the time period over which you are planning into fairly equal sections, such as half terms. Choose a topic for each section. Young children benefit from making links between the new ideas they encounter so as you select each topic, think about the time of year in which you plan to do it. A topic about minibeasts will not be very successful in November!

Although each topic will address all the learning areas, some could focus on a specific area. For example, a topic on Growth would lend itself well to activities relating to Knowledge and Understanding of the World. Another topic might particularly encourage the appreciation of stories. Try to make sure that you provide a variety of topics in your long-term plans.

Autumn 1	All about me
Autumn 2	Shapes/Christmas
Spring 1	Nursery rhymes
Spring 2	Growth
Summer 1	Toys
Summer 2	Water

MEDIUM-TERM PLANS

Medium-term plans will outline the contents of a topic in a little more detail. One way to start this process is by brainstorming on a large piece of paper. Work with your team writing down all the activities you can think of which are relevant to the topic. As you do this it may become clear that some activities go well together. Think about dividing them into themes. The topic of Growth for example has themes such as 'Babies', 'Growing up', 'Seeds' and 'Eggs and life-cycles'. At this stage it is helpful to make a chart. Write the theme ideas down the side of the chart and put a different area of learning at the top of each column. Now you can insert your brainstormed ideas and will quickly see where there are gaps. As you complete the chart take account of children's earlier experiences and provide opportunities for them to progress.

Refer back to the *Curriculum Guidance for the Foundation Stage* (2000) and check that you have addressed as many different aspects of it as you can. Once all your medium-term plans are complete make sure that there are no neglected areas.

DAY-TO-DAY PLANS

The plans you make for each day will outline aspects such as:

- resources needed;
- the way in which you might introduce activities;
- the organisation of adult help;
- size of the group;
- timing;
- key vocabulary.

Identify the learning that each activity is intended to promote. Make a note of any assessments or observations that you are likely to carry out. On your plans make notes of activities that were particularly successful, or any changes you would make another time.

Making plans

A FINAL NOTE

Planning should be seen as flexible. Not all groups meet every day, and not all children attend every day. Any part of the plan can be used independently, stretched over a longer period or condensed to meet the needs of any group. You will almost certainly adapt the activities as children respond to them in different ways and bring their own ideas, interests and enthusiasms. The important thing is to ensure that the children are provided with a varied and enjoyable curriculum that meets their individual developing needs.

USING THIS BOOK

- Collect or prepare suggested resources as listed on page 21.

- Read the section which outlines links to the Early Learning Goals (pages 4-7) and explains the rationale for the topic of Growth.

- For each weekly theme two activities are described in detail as an example to help you in your planning and preparation. Key vocabulary, questions and learning opportunities are identified.

- The skills chart on page 23 will help you to see at a glance which aspects of children's development are being addressed as a focus each week.

- As children take part in the Growth topic activities, their learning will progress. 'Collecting evidence' on page 22 explains how you might monitor children's achievements.

- Find out on page 20 how the topic can be brought together in a grand finale involving parents, children and friends.

- There is additional material to support the working partnership of families and children in the form of a 'Home links' page, and a photocopiable parent's page found at the back of the book.

- It is important to appreciate that the ideas presented in this book will only be a part of your planning. Many activities that will be taking place as routine in your group may not be mentioned. For example, it is assumed that sand, dough, water, puzzles, floor toys and large scale apparatus are part of the ongoing pre-school experience, as are the opportunities which increasing numbers of groups are able to offer for children to develop ICT skills. Role-play areas, stories, rhymes and singing, and group discussion times are similarly assumed to be happening each week although they may not be a focus for described activities.

USING THE EARLY LEARNING GOALS

Having chosen your topic and made your medium-term plans you can use the *Curriculum Guidance for the Foundation Stage* (2000) to highlight the key learning opportunities your activities will address. The Early Learning Goals are split into six areas: Personal, Social and Emotional Development; Communication, Language and Literacy; Mathematical Development; Knowledge and Understanding of the World; Physical Development and Creative Development. Do not expect each of your topics to cover every goal but your long-term plans should allow for all of them to be addressed by the time a child enters Year 1.

The following section highlights parts of the *Curriculum Guidance for the Foundation Stage* in point form to show what children are expected to be able to do in each area of learning by the time they enter Year 1. These points will be used throughout this book to show how activities for a topic on Growth link to these expectations. For example, Personal, Social and Emotional Development point 7 is 'form good relationships with adults and peers'. Activities suggested which provide the opportunity for children to do this will have the reference PS7. This will enable you to see which parts of the Early Learning Goals are covered in a given week and plan for areas to be revisited and developed.

In addition, you can ensure that activities offer variety in the goals to be encountered. Often a similar activity may be carried out to achieve different learning objectives. For example, during this topic the children will work in pairs to create mini-gardens. The children will be developing aspects of Physical Development as they handle tools carefully to plant seeds and make fences and paths. They will also be gaining Knowledge and Understanding of the World as they look closely at plants and Personal, Social and Emotional Development as they cooperate with each other in pairs.

PERSONAL, SOCIAL AND EMOTIONAL DEVELOPMENT (PS)

This area of learning covers important aspects of development that affect the way children learn, behave and relate to others.

By the end of the Foundation Stage, most children will:

PS1 continue to be interested, excited and motivated to learn

PS2 be confident to try activities, initiate ideas and speak in a familiar group

PS3 maintain attention, concentrate and sit quietly when appropriate

PS4 have a developing awareness of their own needs, views and feelings and be sensitive to the needs, views and feelings of others

PS5 have a developing respect for their own cultures and beliefs and those of other people

PS6 respond to significant experiences, showing a range of feelings when appropriate

PS7 form good relationships with adults and peers

PS8 work as a part of a group or class, taking turns and sharing fairly, understanding that there needs to be agreed values and codes of behaviour for groups of people, including adults and children, to work together harmoniously

PS9 understand what is right, what is wrong, and why

PS10 dress and undress independently and manage their own personal hygiene

PS11 select and use activities and resources independently

PS12 consider the consequences of their words and actions for themselves and others

PS13 understand that people have different needs, views, cultures and beliefs, that need to be treated with respect

PS14 understand that they can expect others to treat their needs, views, cultures and beliefs with respect

The topic of Growth provides valuable opportunities for children to develop awareness of their own needs and the needs of others. Time spent discussing caring for plants and other living things will encourage children to speak in a group, to share their feelings and to consider consequences. By playing circle games children will learn to take turns and to listen to each other. Many of the areas outlined above will also be covered as children carry out the activities in other key areas. For example, when children play physical games and join in songs and rhymes they will also have the opportunity to develop PS8.

COMMUNICATION, LANGUAGE AND LITERACY (L)

The objectives set out in the *National Literacy Strategy: Framework for Teaching* for the Reception year are in line with these goals. By the end of the Foundation Stage, most children will be able to:

L1 enjoy listening to and using spoken and written language, and readily turn to it in their play and learning

L2 explore and experiment with sounds, words and texts

L3 listen with enjoyment and respond to stories, songs and other music, rhymes and poems and make up their own stories, songs, rhymes and poems

L4 use language to imagine and recreate roles and experiences

L5 use talk to organise, sequence and clarify thinking, ideas, feelings and events

L6 sustain attentive listening, responding to what they have heard by relevant comments, questions or actions

L7 interact with others, negotiating plans and activities and taking turns in conversation

L8 extend their vocabulary, exploring the meaning and sounds of new words

L9 retell narratives in the correct sequence, drawing on language patterns of stories

L10 speak clearly and audibly with confidence and control and show awareness of the listener, for example by their use of conventions such as greetings, 'please' and 'thank-you'

L11 hear and say initial and final sounds in words and short vowel sounds within words

L12 link sounds to letters, naming and sounding letters of the alphabet

L13 read a range of familiar and common words and simple sentences independently

L14 show an understanding of the elements of stories such as main character, sequence of events, and openings, and how information can be found in non-fiction texts to answer questions about where, who, why and how

L15 know that print carries meaning, and in English, is read from left to right and top to bottom

L16 attempt writing for different purposes, using features of different forms such as lists, stories and instructions

L17 write their own names and other things such as labels and captions and begin to form sentences, sometimes using punctuation

L18 use their phonic knowledge to write simple regular words and make phonetically plausible attempts at more complex words

L19 use a pencil and hold it effectively to form recognisable letters, most of which are correctly formed

There is a wide range of quality fiction and non-fiction books that feature the subject of growing. Several of the activities suggested for the theme of Growth are based on well-known picture books and stories, retelling stories, using drama and reinforcing and extending their vocabulary. Making invitations for grandparent's day will help children to develop their early writing skills. Throughout the topic, opportunities are given for children to explore the sounds of words and to see some of their ideas recorded in pictures, words and on tape. Role-play areas are described that will allow children to use their imagination as they look after babies at the clinic and buy and sell plants at the garden centre.

MATHEMATICAL DEVELOPMENT (M)

The key objectives in the *National Numeracy Strategy: Framework for Teaching* for the Reception year are in line with these goals. By the end of the Foundation Stage, most children should be able to:

M1   say and use number names in order in familiar contexts

M2   count reliably up to ten everyday objects

M3   recognise numerals one to nine

M4   use language such as 'more' or 'less' to compare two numbers

M5   in practical activities and discussion begin to use the vocabulary involved in adding and subtracting

M6   find one more or one less than a number from one to ten.

M7   begin to relate addition to combining two groups of objects and subtraction to 'taking away'

M8   talk about, recognise and recreate simple patterns

M9   use language such as 'circle' or 'bigger' to describe the shape and size of solid and flat shapes

M10   use everyday words to describe position

M11   use developing mathematical ideas and methods to solve practical problems

M12   use language such as 'greater', 'smaller', 'heavier' or 'lighter' to compare quantities

The theme of Growth provides a meaningful context for mathematical activities. Sorting and counting skills are used to play number games with flowerpots and plastic animals. There are several fun activities introducing measurement; height of children and plants; length of caterpillars and weight of babies. Simple money skills are developed in the role-play garden centre. There are also opportunities for children to recognise numbers and shapes as they build number towers, shape giants and use counting rhymes.

KNOWLEDGE AND UNDERSTANDING OF THE WORLD (K)

By the end of the Foundation Stage, most children will be able to:

K1   investigate objects and materials by using all of their senses as appropriate

K2   find out about, and identify, some features of living things, objects and events they observe

K3   look closely at similarities, differences, patterns and change

K4   ask questions about why things happen and how things work

K5   build and construct with a wide range of objects, selecting appropriate resources and adapting their work where necessary

K6   select the tools and techniques they need to shape, assemble and join materials they are using

K7   find out about and identify the uses of everyday technology and use information and communication technology and programmable toys to support their learning

K8   find out about past and present events in their own lives, and those of their families and other people they know

K9   observe, find out about and identify features in the place they live and the natural world

K10 begin to know about their own cultures and beliefs and those of other people

K11 find out about their environment, and talk about those features they like and dislike

The Growth theme offers many opportunities for children to make observations, and find out about the natural world. There are activities to investigate what children and plants need to grow, which creatures lay eggs, and to observe first hand the growth of vegetables, flowers, fruit, caterpillars and so on. As they compare themselves as babies with the present day the children will look closely at similarities, differences and change. Throughout all these activities children should be given the chance to talk about their experiences and ask questions.

PHYSICAL DEVELOPMENT(PD)

By the end of the Foundation Stage, most children will be able to:

PD1 move with confidence, imagination and in safety

PD2 move with control and coordination

PD3 show awareness of space, of themselves and of others

PD4 recognise the importance of keeping healthy and those things which contribute to this

PD5 recognise the changes that happen to their bodies when they are active

PD6 use a range of small and large equipment

PD7 travel around, under, over and through balancing and climbing equipment

PD8 handle tools, objects, construction and malleable materials safely and with increasing control

Activities such as making ladders from construction toys, handling garden tools, using tweezers to sort seeds, and bouncing and throwing balls offer experience of PD8. Pushing dolls' pushchairs around an obstacle course and having wheelbarrow races in

pairs will develop control and coordination. As children join in the keep-fit session they will become more aware of how their bodies change when active. Several collaborative games offer opportunities to move with imagination and awareness of space.

CREATIVE DEVELOPMENT (C)

By the end of the Foundation Stage, most children will be able to:

C1   explore colour, texture, shape, form and space in two or three dimensions

C2   recognise and explore how sounds can be changed, sing simple songs from memory, recognise repeated sounds and sound patterns and match movements to music

C3   respond in a variety of ways to what they see, hear, smell, touch and feel

C4   use their imagination in art and design, music, dance, imaginative and role play and stories

C5   express and communicate their ideas, thoughts and feelings by using a widening range of materials, suitable tools, imaginative and role play, movement, designing and making, and a variety of songs and musical instruments

During this topic children will experience working with a variety of materials as they make baby mobiles, clay handprints, peg butterflies, and salt dough animals. They will be able to develop painting skills to create pictures of the frog's life-cycle, and experiment by blowing paint through straws. C2 and C5 are explored as the children sing lullabies and use musical instruments to make sounds grow louder and quieter, repeat rhythm patterns and accompany songs. Throughout all the activities children are encouraged to talk about what they see and feel as they communicate their ideas in painting, collage, music and drama.

WEEK 1
BABIES

PERSONAL, SOCIAL AND EMOTIONAL DEVELOPMENT

● Invite a mum and new baby to visit. Remind the children to sit quietly, watch and listen as the baby has a bath. Help children to ask questions about what the baby needs. Make a list of ways to help at home with a new baby. (PS2, 3, 7, 8)

● At circle time talk about baby brothers and sisters. Read *Rosie's Babies* by Martin Waddell (Walker) or *Big Brother, Little Brother* by Penny Dale (Walker). Pass a baby doll around the circle and ask children to pretend it is their baby sister or brother. What do they like about the baby? (PS2, 4, 6)

● Ask children to bring in photos of themselves as babies. Can they write their own name as a label? Talk about naming ceremonies in different cultures. (PS4, 5, 6)

COMMUNICATION, LANGUAGE AND LITERACY

● Make a baby clinic in the role-play area, with baby dolls, clothes, bath, nappies, weighing scales, and so on. Prepare record cards for the dolls to include information on weight, injections, and sickness. (L1, 4, 16)

● Sing 'Pat a cake, pat a cake, baker's man'. Clap the rhythm. Play it with a partner. Make a collection of words beginning with 'b'. (L1, 3, 11)

● Make thank-you cards for the new baby and parent who visited. Help children to write simple messages and their own names. Paint portraits of the baby having a bath. (L17, 18, 19)

MATHEMATICAL DEVELOPMENT

● Mark the heights of the children on a wall chart at the beginning of the topic. Measure them again in week six to see who has grown the most. Use lots of mathematical language. (M11)

● Cut up cardboard tubes into hoops. Paint them different colours and add numbers one to ten. Ask children to build number towers. (M1, 3)

KNOWLEDGE AND UNDERSTANDING OF THE WORLD

● 'See how I've grown' (see activity below). (K3, 8)

● Talk about babies teething and milk teeth. Cook some peeled apples in a saucepan. Compare eating slices of raw apple with the apple puree. Taste other fruit purees sold as baby foods. Can the children identify the flavours? (K1, 3, 4)

PHYSICAL DEVELOPMENT

● Make an obstacle course for children to crawl around like babies. Can they push dolls' pushchairs around the same course? (PD1, 2, 7)

● Hold a keep-fit session to music (see activity opposite). (PD2, 4, 5)

CREATIVE DEVELOPMENT

● Sing 'Rock a bye baby'. Ask children to sing the words in a gentle, soothing way while rocking a baby doll or soft toy. Try singing this and other lullabies to the baby visitor.

● Make a baby mobile. Use card templates of teddy bears or moon and stars and paint both sides with black and white geometrical patterns. Suspend from a hoop or clothes hanger. (C1, 5)

ACTIVITY: SEE HOW I'VE GROWN...

Learning opportunity: Observing growth and talking about change.

Early Learning Goal: Knowledge and Understanding

then I was a baby I could...	now I am... I can ...	when I am... I will ...

of the World. Children will be able to look closely at similarities, differences, patterns and change and find out about past and present events in their own lives, and those of their families.

Resources: *See How I Grow* by Angela Wilkes (Dorling Kindersley) or similar book on child's growth; photographs of children when they were babies (see PSED); paper; pencils; crayons.

Organisation: Whole group introduction with small group recording activity.

Key vocabulary: Baby, grow, change, month, when, now.

WHAT TO DO:

Read the book to the whole group. Talk about what the baby learns to do as it grows, such as smile, sit up, play, feed itself, and so on.

Look at the photographs of the children in your group when they were small babies. What can they do now that they could not do then? Make a list of all the changes they have noticed.

In a small group, ask children to record their ideas on a 'then and now' writing frame (see diagram above) to help consolidate their learning. Encourage children to think about what they might be able to do when they are a year older. Can they add this to their picture?

ACTIVITY: KEEP - FIT

Learning opportunity: Listening to instructions and moving to music.

Early Learning Goal: Physical Development. Children will be able to move with control and coordination. They will recognise the importance of keeping healthy and those things which contribute to this and recognise the changes that happen to their bodies when they are active.

Resources: Suitable music with a regular dance beat; CD or tape recorder; large space.

Organisation: Whole group.

Key vocabulary: Keep-fit, exercise, warm-up, stretch, march, bend, stamp, forwards, backwards, left, right.

WHAT TO DO:

Explain to the children that healthy bodies need exercise to keep fit and grow strong. Ask them to watch carefully, listen to the instructions and copy what you do.

Organise children into rows so that they can all see you clearly. Start with a gentle warm-up such as marching up and down on the spot, swinging arms, and bending elbows and knees in time to the beat of the music. Ask children to stretch up tall and out to the sides to really stretch their muscles.

Make up a simple pattern of movement for them to copy such as four steps forwards, four steps back, four to the right, four to the left. If you aim to do four of each action you should keep with the music!

Try some partner work. Children choose a partner and clap each other's hands. End by joining hands in a big circle and walk or skip round. Most important – have fun! Make sure you take some photographs.

After the exercise ask children to put their hands on their chests and feel their hearts beating. Can they identify any other changes in their bodies? Lie down and relax to cool down.

DISPLAY

For fun, put up baby photographs of the adults who work in the setting under the heading 'Where are they now?' Can the children or their parents recognise anyone?

Display photographs of the children when they were babies with the name labels and if possible some taken this week during the keep-fit session. Make a collection of baby books, such as board books, touchy-feely, fabric books and baby toys. Hang the children's baby mobiles above the display.

WEEK 2

GROWING UP

PERSONAL, SOCIAL AND EMOTIONAL DEVELOPMENT

● Read *Once There Were Giants* by Martin Waddell (Walker). Talk with the children about growing up. (PS1, 2, 7)

● Organise a grandparent's day (see activity below). (PS4, 8, 13)

COMMUNICATION, LANGUAGE AND LITERACY

● Write invitations for grandparent's day. Help children to fill in the names of their grandparents and to sign their own name. (If grandparents don't live near enough to visit they might like to invite elderly neighbours.) (L16, 17)

● Read *I Want to Be* by Tony Ross (Collins) (see activity opposite). (L3, 4, 5, 16)

● Ask children to bring in photos of different family members: mum, dad, babies, siblings, grandparents. Talk about the pictures and sort them into babies, children, teenagers, grown-ups and senior citizens. Stick them onto a wall chart with the youngest at the bottom. (L6, 10)

MATHEMATICAL DEVELOPMENT

● Read *Titch* by Pat Hutchins (Red Fox). Use lots of mathematical language to compare sizes of children: height, shoe sizes, length of hair and so on. Look at baby clothes and clothes that are too big. Measure clothes against children for fun. (M9, 11)

● Draw round or make prints of children's hands. Use rulers to measure and compare sizes. Who has got the biggest hands? Use hand spans to measure length. (M3, 4, 9)

● Make a shape giant. Cut out and paint lots of different sized shapes. On a large floor space help children to assemble the shapes into a huge giant to mount on the wall. (M1, 9, 10)

KNOWLEDGE AND UNDERSTANDING OF THE WORLD

● Read *Avocado Baby* by John Burningham (Red Fox). Talk about eating healthy food to help make bones grow strong. Which food is good for growth? Make a chart to show healthy food and foods that are not so good for us. (K2, 4)

● See if children can find out when they got their first tooth, started to walk, spoke their first word, started nursery and so on. Use a tape recorder to help the children record the information. Include stories about funny things they said or did. (K1, 2, 3, 7)

PHYSICAL DEVELOPMENT

● Play the 'Growing up' game. Shout 'Babies' – children have to crawl around the room; 'Toddlers' – walk slowly and unsteadily; 'Children' – run fast; 'Teenagers' – stretch up as tall as possible; 'Grown-ups' – sit down and have a rest! (PD1, 2, 3)

● Use different construction toys to make ladders. Use small world people or small soft toys to climb up the ladders. Ask children to climb ladders on a climbing frame or slide until they are as tall as a grown-up. How does the world look from up there? (PD6, 8)

CREATIVE DEVELOPMENT

● Make clay handprints. Mount on felt base and give to parents as a keepsake. (C5)

● Enjoy making sounds 'grow'. Invite children to select musical instruments. Sit in a circle and ask children to join in one by one and add their sound so the music grows louder. Can they make it grow quieter? Try making sounds grow longer and shorter as well. (C2, 4)

● Build tall tower blocks using junk materials. How tall can you make your tower grow? (C4, 5)

ACTIVITY: GRANDPARENT'S DAY

Learning opportunity: Working together to plan a special day to share with grandparents.

Early Learning Goal: Personal, Social and Emotional Development. Children will be able to work as part of a group, taking turns and sharing fairly. They will understand that people have different needs, views, cultures and beliefs, that need to be treated with respect.

Resources: Grandparents or older friends; ingredients for food to be cooked; songs and rhymes from *Tinderbox* and *This Little Puffin* (see Resources).

Organisation: Whole group. Cooking activities with small group.

Key vocabulary: Growing, age, old, young, names of grandparents.

WHAT TO DO:

Talk to children about growing up and getting old. Explain that older people have lived for longer and learned lots about the world.

On grandparent's day children can invite their grandparents to come and see what they do at nursery. Ask visitors to bring in something special from when they were young to show the children, such as a photo, book or toy.

Talk about what the visitors may like to eat and drink. Bake biscuits or scones with the children. Help them to write out menus for the day so their guests can choose. Learn some songs and rhymes to share on the day. 'Slowly, slowly walks my grandad' from *Tinderbox* and 'These are grandmother's glasses' *(This Little Puffin)* always go down well.

On the day, encourage children to show grandparents around and invite them to join in creative activities. Put out chairs so visitors can sit down and share books with the children. Ask children to serve food and drink to their grandparents.

Set aside a time when grandparents can share any items or memories with the children of when they were small.

ACTIVITY: WHEN I GROW UP...

Learning opportunity: Talking, drawing and writing about themselves.

Early Learning Goal: Communication, Language and Literacy. Children will be able to listen with enjoyment and respond to stories and use language to imagine and recreate roles and experiences.

Resources: *I Want to Be* by Tony Ross (Collins); paper; pencils; crayons.

Organisation: Small group.

Key vocabulary: Vocabulary from book, grown-up, occupations chosen by children.

WHAT TO DO:

Read the story to the children. The little princess wanted to know 'What was the best way to be?' Talk about being kind, loving, clean, brave, good at swimming, clever and healthy as well as different occupations!

Talk about what the children want to be when they grow up. What different jobs do their mums and dads do? Play a circle game of 'When I grow up I want to be…' with each child adding an idea.

Play a game of 'What's my line?' Invite children to mime a job for the other children to guess. Ask children to draw a picture of themselves in the future. Scribe captions for their pictures. Compile into a group book.

DISPLAY

Make a tower of hands using the handprints. Ask the children to measure how high they are in hands. Cut round drawings of the children's feet and use as footsteps to make trails around the room.

Mount and display photographs of grandparent's day. Ask children to paint or draw portraits of their grandparents to add to the display.

WEEK 3

SEEDS

PERSONAL, SOCIAL AND EMOTIONAL DEVELOPMENT

● Invite a farmer, keen gardener or adult who works with plants to visit and talk about their work. Encourage children to listen attentively and ask relevant questions. (PS2, 3, 7, 8)

● Read *Fran's Flower* by Lisa Bruce (Bloomsbury). Talk about waiting patiently for seeds to grow. What happens when Fran gets fed up of waiting? What do the children find it difficult to wait for? (PS4, 9, 12)

COMMUNICATION, LANGUAGE AND LITERACY

● Read *Jasper's Beanstalk* by Nick Butterworth (Red Fox). Make a story bag containing a toy Jasper, a bean, garden tools, torch and a long beanstalk made from fabric or green crepe paper. Invite children to retell the story. (L3, 4, 9)

● Sing 'I went to the garden' from *This Little Puffin* (see Resources). Make a chart showing the days of the week. Help children to draw up a rota for watering the seeds and plants. (L3, 7, 16)

● Make a collection of words about growing or words that rhyme with 'grow'. Write the word 'growing' on a piece of card cut into the shape of a flowerpot. Ask children to think of words and scribe them onto leaf shapes. How tall will your word plant grow? (L2, 8, 11)

MATHEMATICAL DEVELOPMENT

● Open a garden centre in the role-play area (see activity opposite). (M1, 3, 5, 6)

● Add numbers one to ten to a set of flowerpots. Ask children to put the correct number of flowers in each pot. (M2, 3, 4)

● Read *Ten Seeds* by Ruth Brown (Andersen Press). Act out the story using ten children. (M1, 2, 5)

KNOWLEDGE AND UNDERSTANDING OF THE WORLD

● Help each child to plant and care for a sunflower seed (see activity opposite). (K2, 3, 4, 9)

● Look at the seeds in different fruit such as apples, grapes, peaches, melons, cherries and so on. Try planting them in small pots of compost. Remind the children to be patient (see PSED) as some seeds take a long time to germinate. Make a matching game. Cut out pictures of fruit from magazines and laminate or mount them on card. Match the seeds to the fruit. (K1, 2, 3)

● Investigate what plants need to grow. Plant three pots of seeds: let one dry out, water one, and put the third inside a box with a lid. Help children to record the results. (K2, 3, 4)

PHYSICAL DEVELOPMENT

● Fill the sand tray with compost and provide sieves, spades, trowels, flowerpots and seed trays. Remind the children to wash their hands carefully after playing with the compost. (PD4, 8)

● Fill a seed tray with a collection of seeds, lentils, peas, beans and so on. Ask children to use tweezers to sort out the seed mixture into different containers. (PD8)

● Ask children to curl up into a small body shape like a seed. Encourage them to slowly uncurl and grow as they hear the rain (maracas, rainmaker, tambourine) and sunshine (triangle, jingle bells). (PD1, 2)

CREATIVE DEVELOPMENT

● Tell the story of 'Jack and the Beanstalk'. Act it out dramatically. Make a giant beanstalk with twisted newspaper, green crepe paper leaves. Suspend it from the ceiling for children to pretend to climb. (C4, 5)

● Learn this sunflower song:

I'm a yellow sunflower

Strong and tall

See my petals

See my stalk

When I feel the sunshine I will grow

Taller and taller and taller I go.

(Tune: 'I'm a little teapot') (C2)

● Make observational drawings of flowers and plants using coloured pencils and pastels. (C1)

ACTIVITY: GARDEN CENTRE

Learning opportunity: Using number skills to buy and sell garden items.

Early Learning Goal: Mathematical Development. Children will be able to count reliably up to ten everyday objects and recognise numerals one to nine. They will begin to use the vocabulary involved in adding and subtracting.

Resources: A role-play area set out as a garden centre with flowers, plants (real and artificial), seed packets, flowerpots, seed trays, tools, buckets, spades, garden gloves, boots, watering cans; real coins (1p, 2p, 5p, 10p); card; felt pens; tissue paper; egg boxes; paint; straws; a till; baskets.

Organisation: Whole group introduction with small group using the area.

Key vocabulary: Garden centre, price, money, how much, add, take away.

WHAT TO DO:

Involve children in setting up a garden centre in the role-play area. Talk about any garden centres that the children have visited.

Let the children make cut flowers to sell using different materials. Use small plastic flowerpots filled with scrunched-up tissue paper and painted flowers. Make seed packets using pictures from garden catalogues. Label goods using 1p, 2p, 5p, 10p. Help children to write simple shopping lists.

Introduce the area to the whole group and talk about the different roles of buying, selling and looking after stock. Choose a small group to play in the garden centre. Set challenges. Can you buy one more flower? How many have you got now?

ACTIVITY: GROWING SUNFLOWERS

Learning opportunity: Planting and caring for seeds.

Early Learning Goal: Knowledge and Understanding of the World. Children will be able to find out about, and identify, some features of living things they observe. They will look closely at similarities, differences, patterns and change, and ask questions about why things happen and how things work.

Resources: *A Seed in Need* by Sam Godwin (MacDonald Young); sunflower seeds; plastic cups; compost; water; droppers; lolly sticks; paper; pencils; camera.

Organisation: Whole group.

Key vocabulary: Plant, seed, shoot, root, bud, grow.

WHAT TO DO:

Read *A Seed in Need* (see Resources) to the children. What does the seed need to grow? Explain to the children that they are each going to plant a sunflower seed and care for it.

Help children to fill cups with compost, push a finger down into the soil and plant a seed. Explain that the plants need to be watered regularly. Ask children to write their name on a lollystick and label their plant. During the next few weeks children should observe the changes as the seeds grow and send up shoots. Record the changes in a sequence of pictures and photographs.

Ask for a volunteer to be drawn round on a length of paper. Paint in clothes and features and cut out the shape. Mount the picture on the wall with the feet level with the flowerpots. Which plant will be first to grow as tall as a child?

DISPLAY

Create a greenhouse in the display corner. Display some of the plants that the children are growing on a table. Make a backdrop using fruit and vegetable printing. Add the observational drawings of flowers and plants.

WEEK 4

GROWING TALL

PERSONAL, SOCIAL AND EMOTIONAL DEVELOPMENT

● Talk about plants that grow to provide us with food and drink. Make a list. Talk about harvest celebrations when we say thank-you for our food and the farmers who grow it. (PS1, 4, 5, 8)

● Grow cherry tomatoes in grow-bags around the nursery. Encourage children to taste the tomatoes even if they are new to them. (PS2, 4, 8)

COMMUNICATION, LANGUAGE AND LITERACY

● Sing the nursery rhyme 'Mary, Mary, quite contrary'. Help children to design a garden. Which plants and flowers will they choose? Ask children to draw a plan of their garden. Change the words of the rhyme to describe a child's garden. (L3, 4, 16)

● How many different flowers and plants can the children name? Make a colourful chart to hang in the garden centre, or a plant alphabet using gardening catalogues. (L2, 8, 12)

● Sprinkle cress or grass seeds onto damp paper towels in the shape of a child's initial letter and wait for them to grow. (L11)

MATHEMATICAL DEVELOPMENT

● Make a collection of flowerpots. Ask children to sort them according to size. (M2, 9)

● Provide each child with a drawing of flowers made by drawing round a coin a number of times. Put coloured counters on each circle. Play a game in which children take turns to throw a dice and pick the same number of petals. (M2, 5, 8)

● Make a number line using fingerprint flowers. (M3)

● Cut out pictures of plants and mount on card. Using small cubes, ask children to measure how tall the plants are. Which is the tallest plant? (M2, 4, 9)

KNOWLEDGE AND UNDERSTANDING OF THE WORLD

● Make a mini-vegetable garden. Cut the top 2.5cm off a carrot, parsnip, beetroot or pineapple and place in a pebble-filled dish topped up with water. Help children to keep the plants watered and watch them grow. (K1, 2)

● Plant broad beans in glass jars around blotting paper and observe the growth. When the roots and shoots have grown a little turn some of the jars upside down. What do the children think will happen? (K2, 3, 4)

● Place cut celery sticks in water and food colouring and observe what happens. Make cross sections of the celery for the children to draw. (K2, 3, 4)

PHYSICAL DEVELOPMENT

● Plant a mini-garden in a seed tray (see activity opposite). (PD6, 8)

● Play a game of 'Roots and shoots'. Sing this song to the tune of 'The wise man built his house upon the rock':

The roots grow down and the shoots grow up (three times)

And the plant stands firm and tall.

● Ask children to choose a partner and make wheelbarrows. Enjoy races up and down the room. Set out obstacles for the children to go round. (PD1, 2, 3, 7)

CREATIVE DEVELOPMENT

● Enjoy learning the chant and adding actions and percussion instruments to 'The Enormous Turnip' from *Three Singing Pigs* (see Resources). (C5)

● Make a group collage (see activity opposite). (C1)

● Learn action rhymes 'Five fat peas in a pea pod pressed' and 'I had a little cherry stone' from *This Little Puffin* (see Resources). (C2, 4)

ACTIVITY: GROW A MINI-GARDEN

Learning opportunity: Designing and planting a mini-garden.

Early Learning Goal: Physical Development. Children will be able to handle tools, objects, and malleable materials with increasing control.

Resources: Seed trays; shoebox lids lined with silver foil; compost; plants; moss; turf; stones; shells; film containers; flowers; water; twigs.

Organisation: Small group.

Key vocabulary: Plant, dig, spread, corner, cover, cut, layer, names of chosen materials.

WHAT TO DO:

Explain that they are going to work in pairs to create a mini-garden. Show them the different materials available (see Resources). Help children to work together to plan their garden.

Ask children to bring in items from home to use. Fill seed trays or lids with compost. Use sprinkled gravel for paths and shiny foil trays for ponds. Cut pieces of turf or moss for lawns and put small cut flowers in film containers full of water. Use twigs for winter trees, and small plants for bushes. Make fences out of lolly sticks or card. Encourage careful handling of delicate materials.

Remind children to care for and water the mini-gardens. Organise a time for parents to come and view the children's work.

ACTIVITY: A TREE FOR ALL SEASONS

Learning opportunity: Working together to make a group collage using a variety of materials.

Early Learning Goal: Creative Development. Children will be able to explore colour, texture, shape, form and space in two and three dimensions.

Resources: Pictures or photographs of different trees from fiction and non-fiction books; paper; paint; selection of scraps of material; glue; scissors; tissue paper; twigs; coloured paper.

Organisation: Small group.

Key vocabulary: Spring, summer, autumn, winter.

WHAT TO DO:

Talk about the seasons of the year. Look at pictures of trees in books and magazines. How can you tell which season it is from the trees? Talk about spring blossom, summer fruit, changing autumn colours and falling leaves and bare winter branches.

Explain to the children that you are going to make a group collage to show the changes to a cherry or apple tree in each season. Let children choose which season they would like to work on. Decide on a basic shape for the tree.

Ask each group to select suitable materials for their tree. Spring - pink or white tissue paper or material for blossom, fluffy white clouds in sky. Summer – shiny red paper cherries or apples, blue sky and warm sun. Autumn – coloured paper or material leaves on the tree and the ground. Winter – bare twigs and white painted snow on the ground.

DISPLAY

Make giant sunflowers using circles cut from thin yellow card (see diagram) and sunflower seeds. Mount them on the wall and paint on stems and leaves. Display the real sunflowers, mini-vegetable and mini-gardens on the table.

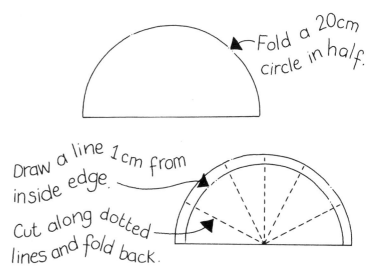

Fold a 20cm circle in half.

Draw a line 1cm from inside edge.

Cut along dotted lines and fold back.

WEEK 5

EGGS AND LIFE-CYCLES

PERSONAL, SOCIAL AND EMOTIONAL DEVELOPMENT

● Talk to children about looking after living creatures. Set up the butterfly garden (see Knowledge and Understanding of the World), a fish tank or a tank of frogspawn.

● Make a collection of picture books about animals that lay eggs or have interesting life-cycles such as *If at First You Do Not See* by Ruth Brown (Scholastic), *Who Am I?* by Judith Nicholls (Ladybird) and *Daisy and the Egg* by Jane Simmons (Orchard). Talk about how it would feel to be one of these creatures. (PS2, 4, 8)

● Tell the story of 'The Ugly Duckling' by Hans Christian Andersen. How should the other animals have behaved to the ugly duckling? (PS2, 4, 9)

COMMUNICATION, LANGUAGE AND LITERACY

● Read *The Very Hungry Caterpillar* by Eric Carle (Puffin). Make a circular concertina caterpillar diary showing the different stages and retelling the story. (L3, 14, 15, 16)

● Make name caterpillars. Give each child as many card circles as there are letters in their name. Help them to write their initial letter on one and then scribe the other letters. Thread the circles together using coloured string. Draw a funny face on the first circle. (L11, 12, 17)

MATHEMATICAL DEVELOPMENT

● Make caterpillars out of Plasticine or playdough. Who has made the longest one? How can they make it grow longer? Use cubes or rulers to measure the length of the caterpillars. (M1, 9, 11)

● Play 'Caterpillars and butterflies' (see activity opposite). (M2, 3, 7, 10)

● Use templates to draw round lots of different sized circles. Use a pencil, string and a drawing pin as a compass to draw large circles. Compare the circle shape with an egg shape. (M9, 11)

KNOWLEDGE AND UNDERSTANDING OF THE WORLD

● Observe the life-cycle of the caterpillar by using the butterfly garden (see Resources). The kit contains five caterpillars, food, hatching house and full instructions. (K1, 2, 3, 4)

● Invite children to use magnifying glasses when observing the minibeasts. Talk about the way in which they make things look larger. (K1, 2)

● Investigate which creatures lay eggs (see activity opposite). (K2, 3, 9)

● Ask each child to cut a white circle into four strips. Stick these down on a piece of black sugar paper leaving a gap between each piece and watch the circle grow into a 'stretchy egg'! (K5, 6)

PHYSICAL DEVELOPMENT

● Make up a life-cycle dance. Divide children into four groups: eggs, caterpillars, chrysalides, and butterflies. Talk about how each group could move. Eggs - curl up small, slowly stretching out as they hatch; caterpillars – crawl, wriggle, eat and grow; chrysalides – spin and then stay still; butterflies – fly around room. Make up a story and give each group an opportunity to dance. Use recorded music or percussion instruments. (PD1, 2, 3)

● Use playdough or clay to make the different stages of the caterpillar life-cycle. (PD8)

CREATIVE DEVELOPMENT

● Working in pairs or small groups, paint the life-cycle of the frog. Print white circles and add black specks to make frogspawn. Cut tadpole shapes out of black sugar paper. Make collage frogs out of green paper, material, and paint. (C5)

● Make a giant woven caterpillar. Wrap string or wool around paper plates and weave thin strips of fabric and ribbon through the wool warp. (C1)

● Use old-fashioned clothes pegs, tissue paper, fabric, and pipe cleaners to make peg butterflies. Paint stripes on the peg body. (C5)

● Sing 'Tiny caterpillar' from *Bobby Shaftoe, Clap Your Hands* (see Resources). (C2)

ACTIVITY: CATERPILLARS AND BUTTERFLIES

Learning opportunity: Playing a game using numbers and positional language.

Early Learning Goal: Mathematical Development. Children will be able to count reliably and recognise numerals one to nine. They will use everyday words to describe position.

Resources: A game board consisting of squares 1–30, with caterpillars, butterflies, and chrysalides (like snakes and ladders); one dice; four plastic caterpillars as game counters.

Organisation: Small group.

Key vocabulary: Numbers one to nine, add, caterpillar, butterfly, chrysalis, down, up, miss a turn.

WHAT TO DO:

Show the children the game board. Explain that they need to take turns to roll the dice and move the caterpillars or counters along the board and follow these rules. If they land on a caterpillar's head they slide down to the tail. If they land on a butterfly's body they can fly up to its head. If they land on a chrysalis they have to stay still and miss a turn. Which caterpillar will be first to reach the last square of the board and successfully grow into a butterfly?

Ask the children to count and move the plastic caterpillars accurately. Encourage the use of positional language. Older children could use two dice and develop addition skills.

ACTIVITY: WHAT'S HATCHING?

Learning opportunity: Investigating how many different creatures lay eggs.

Early Learning Goal: Knowledge and Understanding of the World. Children will be able to find out about and identify some features of living things, objects and events they observe and look closely at similarities, differences, patterns and change.

Resources: Non-fiction books; pictures; photographs; encyclopaedias; access to a computer; card; pens.

Organisation: Whole group.

Key vocabulary: Egg, hatching, bird, reptile, insects, amphibians, fish.

WHAT TO DO:

Explain that they are going to make a classification chart about creatures that lay eggs. Cut out a large egg shape from card and draw a jagged crack across the middle. Help children make a list of all the different families of creatures that lay eggs including birds, reptiles, amphibians, insects and fish. Talk in simple terms about the differences between these groups. Write the names of the different groups on suitably shaped pieces of card and hang them from the giant egg.

Provide children with books, magazines, CD-Roms and other resources to find pictures of all these animals. Ask them to cut out or draw as many different creatures to illustrate the chart. Can the children sort the pictures into birds, reptiles, insects and so on?

DISPLAY

Make a themed display with the giant woven caterpillar surrounded by mini-name caterpillars and peg butterflies. Ask children to sponge-print multi-coloured caterpillars to use as a background.

Ask the children about their favourite food and create a frieze showing a new version of *The Hungry Caterpillar* and what they think he might like to eat.

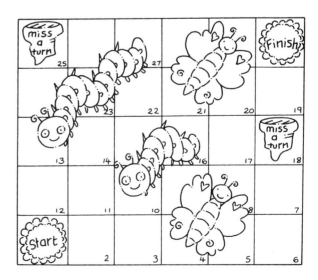

WEEK 6

ANIMAL BABIES

PERSONAL, SOCIAL AND EMOTIONAL DEVELOPMENT

● Invite a local vet or farmer to talk to the children about caring for young animals. Plan with the children the questions they might like to ask. Have any of the children's pets had babies that they could bring in to show? Check children's records for any allergies or fears. (PS3, 4, 7)

● Read *Emma's Lamb* by Kim Lewis (Walker). Emma has to return the lamb to its mother. Talk about how animals and children need their parents to look after them. (PS4, 9)

● Talk about the garden party that will take place this week. What preparations do the children need to make? Discuss food and make invitations. (PS1, 2, 8)

COMMUNICATION, LANGUAGE AND LITERACY

● Help children to think of names or words to describe baby animals beginning with the same initial letter, for instance Katie's kitten, lonely lamb, and so on. Use these as characters in made-up stories. Paint pictures of these characters. (L1, 2, 11, 12)

● Add a new pet or baby animal corner to the garden centre. Use soft toys and cages. Help children to make posters advertising this new feature. Research information from non-fiction books about caring for baby animals. Make leaflets to give to new pet owners. (L4, 7, 14, 16)

● Play 'Family pairs' (see activity below). (L2, 3,8)

MATHEMATICAL DEVELOPMENT

● Make a number frieze showing different numbers of baby animals: Mum – one baby; sheep – two lambs; dog – three puppies; cat – four kittens; rabbit – five kittens; pig – ten piglets, and so on. (M2, 3, 4)

● Make a collection of plastic animals and sort them into families. Give the children some fields cut from green card with numbers marked on them. Can they put the right number of lambs in one field? (M2, 3, 5, 6)

● Don't forget to measure how much the children have grown since week one. Who has grown the most? (M4, 9)

KNOWLEDGE AND UNDERSTANDING OF THE WORLD

● Read *What's it Like to be a Baby Elephant?* (see Resources). Ask the children to imagine the life of a baby elephant or other animal. How does it compare with the children's lives? Are there any things that all babies need? (K3, 9)

● Make flower-shaped biscuits and egg and cress sandwiches for the garden party. Talk about ingredients and how they change from raw to cooked. (K3, 4, 6)

PHYSICAL DEVELOPMENT

● If possible, take a small group on a walk to visit the local pet shop. Ask the shopkeeper to show children any baby animals. Collect any leaflets for the pet corner in the garden centre. (PD1, 4)

● Devise some games to play at the garden party. Remind children of activities and games enjoyed during the Growth topic. (PD1, 6)

CREATIVE DEVELOPMENT

● Play 'Where's my baby?' (see activity opposite). (C2, 3, 4)

● Use salt dough and different-sized animal cutters to make animal families. (C5)

● Make hats to wear at the garden party decorated with tissue paper and material flowers and minibeasts. (C5)

ACTIVITY: FAMILY PAIRS

Learning opportunity: Matching pairs of cards showing young and adult animals, words and pictures. Developing vocabulary and making up stories and rhymes.

Early Learning Goal: Communication, Language and Literacy. Children will be able to listen with enjoyment and respond to stories, rhymes and poems and make up their own stories, rhymes and poems. They will extend their vocabulary, exploring the meaning and sounds of new words.

Resources: Pairs of cards, made or bought, depicting a variety of adult and young animals with pictures and words; soft toys.

Organisation: Small group.

Key vocabulary: Names of animals, pair, family, young, adult, grown-up.

WHAT TO DO:

Talk about animal families and introduce correct terminology such as cat/kitten, horse/foal, lion/cub, goat/kid and so on. Extend children's vocabulary by introducing more unusual pairs such as goose/gosling and kangaroo/joey. Show the children the cards and place them picture down on the table. Help children to take it in turn to match the baby animal with its parent and make 'family pairs'.

Alternatively, deal the cards out between four children. Have they got any family pairs in their hand? Can they make the sound of this animal pair or think of a clue for the other children to guess?

In a larger group, give each child a different animal card or soft toy to hold. Tell a story about as many of the animals as possible. Each time a different animal is mentioned, ask the child holding the card or toy to stand up and make a suitable sound or action and then sit down as quickly as possible. Invite children to make up their own stories or rhymes using as many animals as they can. Record the stories on audiotape and listen back.

ACTIVITY: WHERE'S MY BABY?

Learning opportunity: Recognising and repeating rhythm patterns.

Early Learning Goal: Creative Development. Children will be able to recognise and explore how sounds can be changed, recognise repeated sounds and sound patterns and match movements to music.

Resources: Prepared cards with words, symbols and pictures (see illustration), playful puppies, woolly lambs, kittens, cubs; percussion instruments.

Organisation: Whole group.

Key vocabulary: Animal names, listen, clap, repeat, echo.

WHAT TO DO:

Ask the children to sit in a circle. Clap a simple pattern for the children to copy or echo. It helps if another adult works with the children and helps them to clap the pattern back.

Show the cards for the animal babies and practise saying and clapping each one. Clap the number of dots on the card that matches the syllables in the words. Divide children into four groups, one for each animal, and ask them to stand next to their cards in the four corners of the room. Stand in the centre and pretend to be the mother animal searching for her baby. Ask children to move forwards slowly when they hear you clap their pattern. They must stop moving when you clap the next pattern. Which baby animal will reach the mother first?

Play the game several times so each group gets a turn to win. Ask a confident child to stand in the centre and clap the animal names. This game also works with animal noises such as woof, baa, miaow, and roar.

DISPLAY

Display the children's salt dough animal families and make a collection of books about baby animals. Mount the children's paintings of baby animal characters for parents and friends to view. Help children use IT skills to produce labels for their work.

BRINGING IT ALL TOGETHER

GARDEN PARTY

Talk to the children about the garden party. This could be a simple event during the last hour of a session to which parents, carers and friends can be invited. Alternatively, it could be a fundraising event held over a whole afternoon. At the start of the topic, inform parents of the date of the special event and that you would like plants to sell at the plant stall.

PREPARATION

Explain to the children that the garden party is an opportunity to show things that have been made and grown during the topic and explain what they have learned about growth to their families and friends. Plan and practise with the children a short presentation of some of the rhymes, songs and activities that they have enjoyed during the last few weeks.

Adult help will be vital to the success of this event. Support will be needed in setting up, serving refreshments, taking photographs and helping children to enjoy the activities.

INVITATIONS

Talk about what information will need to be included on the invitations such as date, time and place. Help children make flower-shaped invitations for their friends and family and sign their names.

REFRESHMENTS

Encourage the children to think about what food would be suitable to serve at a garden party. How should the food be presented?

Buy plain paper tablecloths and let children decorate them with printed flower shapes. Put vases of fresh flowers on the tables. Serve the food on flowery plates with doileys.

- Sandwiches filled with egg, home-grown cress, and cucumber (see Week 6).
- Bowls of cherry tomatoes.
- Vegetable crudités – celery, carrots, cucumber, and red pepper.
- Tuna fish dip - blend a tin of tuna fish with 100g of cream cheese and the juice of one lemon.
- Flower-shaped biscuits (see Week 6). Use different coloured icing and decorate with sweets and cake decorations.
- Strawberries and cream.
- Fruit punch - mix together cold tea, apple juice, and slices of fresh fruit. Serve in clear plastic glasses.

PLANT STALL

Ask children and parents to bring in plants from home to sell at the plant stall. Any plants grown by the children can also be included.

Make hand decorated flowerpots to sell at the plant stall. Help children to paint plastic or clay flowerpots using acrylic paints with their own designs.

ACTIVITIES

Children can wear their garden party hats (see Week 6) and help visitors to make their own. Provide a table with suitable materials and make a small charge.

Plan competitions using children's activities from previous weeks such as 'tallest sunflower', 'biggest tomato', 'best mini-garden', or 'most imaginative garden design'.

Hold a treasure hunt. Provide each child with a list of things that are growing for them to spot: pink flower, bird, baby, flowering bush, tall tree, rose, snail, and so on.

Guess the number of carrots in a box?

Guess the weight of the pumpkin?

Guess the height of Sam's dad?

PHOTOGRAPHS

Take photographs of the children with the plants they have grown for proud parents to buy! Put enlarged photographs of the children and their families involved in all the different activities up on display. Let the children help you compose suitable amusing captions for them.

RESOURCES

RESOURCES TO COLLECT

- Toys for role-play baby clinic including baby dolls.
- Baby catalogues and magazines.
- Baby clothes.
- Equipment for role-play garden centre.
- Different sized flowerpots.
- Compost and gardening tools.
- Variety of seeds, beans and plants.
- Magnifying glasses.
- Soft toys for pet corner.
- Plastic animals, young and adult.
- Old-fashioned clothes pegs.

EVERYDAY RESOURCES

- Boxes, large and small, for modelling including cardboard tubes.
- Papers and cards of different weights, colours and textures, such as sugar paper, corrugated card, blotting paper, silver and shiny papers.
- Dry powder paints for mixing, and mixed paints for covering large areas and printing.
- Different sized paintbrushes from household brushes and rollers to thin brushes for intricate work, and a variety of paint mixing containers.
- A variety of drawing and colouring pencils, crayons, pastels and so on.
- Decorative and finishing materials such as sequins, foils, glitter, tinsel, threads, beads, pieces of textiles.
- Construction toys
- Clay, playdough and animal cutters.
- Tape recorder
- Percussion instruments

STORIES

Rosie's Babies by Martin Waddell (Walker).

Big Brother, Little Brother by Penny Dale (Walker).

The Baby's Catalogue by Janet and Allan Ahlberg (Puffin).

Once There Were Giants by Martin Waddell (Walker).

I Want to Be by Tony Ross (Collins).

Titch by Pat Hutchins (Red Fox).

Avocado Baby by John Burningham (Red Fox).

Fran's Flower by Lisa Bruce (Bloomsbury).

Jasper's Beanstalk by Nick Butterworth (Red Fox).

Ten Seeds by Ruth Brown (Andersen Press).

If at First You Do Not See by Ruth Brown (Scholastic).

Who Am I? by Judith Nicholls (Ladybird).

Daisy and the Egg by Jane Simmons (Orchard).

The Very Hungry Caterpillar by Eric Carle (Puffin).

Emma's Lamb by Kim Lewis (Walker).

NON-FICTION

See How I Grow by Angela Wilkes (Dorling Kindersley).

Babies by Henry Pluckrose (Franklin Watts).

A Seed in Need by Sam Godwin (Hodder Wayland).

What's it Like to be a Baby Elephant? by Honor Head (Belitha Press).

Egg – A Photographic Story of Hatching (Dorling Kindersley).

SONGS AND RHYMES

This Little Puffin by Elizabeth Matterson (Puffin).

Bobby Shaftoe, Clap your Hands by Sue Nicholls (A&C Black).

Tinderbox (A&C Black).

Three Singing Pigs by Kaye Umansky (A&C Black).

USEFUL ADDRESSES

The Butterfly Garden from Insect Lore
PO Box 1420
Kiln Farm
Milton Keynes
MK19 6ZH
Tel: 01908 563338
www.insectlore.co.uk

All books were available from leading booksellers at the time of writing.

COLLECTING EVIDENCE OF CHILDREN'S LEARNING

Monitoring children's development is an important task. Keeping a record of children's achievements will help you to see progress and will draw attention to those who are having difficulties for some reason. If a child needs additional professional help, such as speech therapy, your records will provide valuable evidence.

Records should be the result of collaboration between group leaders, parents and carers. Parents should be made aware of your record keeping policies when their child joins your group. Show them the type of records you are keeping and make sure they understand that they have an opportunity to contribute. As a general rule, your records should form an open document. Any parent should have access to records relating to his or her child. Take regular opportunities to talk to parents about children's progress. If you have formal discussions regarding children about whom you have particular concerns, a dated record of the main points should be kept.

KEEPING IT MANAGEABLE

Records should be helpful in informing group leaders, adult helpers and parents and always be for the benefit of the child. However, keeping records of every aspect of each child's development can become a difficult task. The sample shown will help to keep records manageable and useful. The golden rule is to keep them simple.

Observations will basically fall into three categories:

- **Spontaneous records:** Sometimes you will want to make a note of observations as they happen, for example a child is heard counting cars accurately during a play activity, or is seen to play collaboratively for the first time.

- **Planned observations:** Sometimes you will plan to make observations of children's developing skills in their everyday activities.

Using the learning opportunity identified for an activity will help you to make appropriate judgments about children's capabilities and to record them systematically.

To collect information:

- talk to children about their activities and listen to their responses;

- listen to children talking to each other;

- observe children's work such as early writing, drawings, paintings and 3-d models. (Keeping photocopies or photographs is sometimes useful.)

Sometimes you may wish to set up 'one-off' activities for the purposes of monitoring development. Some groups, for example, ask children to make a drawing of themselves at the beginning of each term to record their progressing skills in both coordination and observation. Do not attempt to make records following every activity!

- **Reflective observations:** It is useful to spend regular time reflecting on the progress of a few children (about four children each week). Aim to make some brief comments about each child every half term.

INFORMING YOUR PLANNING

Collecting evidence about children's progress is time-consuming but essential. When you are planning, use the information you have collected to help you to decide what learning opportunities you need to provide next for children. For example, a child who has poor pencil or brush control will benefit from more play with dough or construction toys to build the strength of hand muscles.

Example of recording chart

	Personal, Social and Emotional Development	Communication, Language and Literacy	Mathematical Development	Knowledge and Understanding of the World	Physical Development	Creative Development
Name: Joel McBride			**D.O.B.** 24.7.99		**Date of entry:** 17.9.02	
ONE	Reluctant to leave mum. Enjoyed new baby visit. 30.9.02 EB	Enjoys listening to stories, especially *Jasper's Beanstalk*. Can recognise initial letter of name. 20.10.02 LM	Can say numbers to ten and count accurately five items. Identifies circles. 27.11.02 EB	Interested in plants and living things. Good at making observations. 5.11.02 EB	Lacks confidence on large apparatus. Good use of construction toys. 6.12.02 GS	Enjoys painting and making things. Reluctant to join in musical activities. 20.11.02 EB
TWO						
THREE						

Skills overview of six-week plan

Week	Topic focus	Personal, Social and Emotional Development	Communication, Language and Literacy	Mathematical Development	Knowledge and Understanding of the World	Physical Development	Creative Development
1	Babies	Listening Taking turns Care of others	Role play Book making Initial sounds	Measuring Counting Recognising numbers	Observing change Talking Recording	Moving with control and coordination Recognising body changes	Singing Using materials Painting
2	Growing up	Awareness of needs Planning as a group Dressing skills	Writing for a purpose Listening to stories Talking	Using mathematical language Measuring; Shapes	Investigating Recording Observing change	Moving with imagination and control Using construction	Using different media; Making sounds Modelling
3	Seeds	Listening Discussing feelings	Retelling stories Extending vocabulary	Money; Counting Recognising numbers Subtraction	Observing Comparing Investigating	Using range of equipment Fine motor skills; Moving with control and imagination	Role play; Singing Observational drawing
4	Growing tall	Saying thank you Sharing; Care of others Talking	Writing for a purpose Describing Initial sounds	Sorting; Mathematical language; Recognising numbers; Measuring	Observing; Talking Asking questions Recording	Handling tools Moving with control	Making sounds Using materials Singing
5	Eggs and life-cycles	Care of others Discussing feelings and behaviour	Listening to stories Writing Recognising names	Measuring Mathematical language Counting; Shapes	Observing Investigating Using tools	Moving with imagination and coordination Using malleable materials	Using different media Weaving; Painting Singing
6	Animal babies	Listening Care of others Collaborative planning	Initial letters; Writing for a purpose Making up stories	Using numbers Counting Measuring	Talking; Comparing Observing changes	Moving safely; Using a range of equipment Planning games	Listening and making sounds; Modelling Using materials

HOME LINKS

The theme of Growth lends itself to useful links with children's homes and families. Through working together children and adults gain respect for each other and build comfortable and confident relationships.

ESTABLISHING PARTNERSHIPS

● Keep parents informed about the topic of Growth and the themes for each week. By understanding the work of the group, parents will enjoy the involvement of contributing ideas, time and resources.

● Ask for parental permission before taking children off the premises to visit the pet shop. Additional adult help will be necessary for this activity to be carried out safely.

● Photocopy the parent's page for each child to take home.

● Ask parents for help in inviting grandparents to your grandparent's day.

● Invite friends, carers and families to join in the fun at the garden party.

● Invite parents to take photographs at the grandparent's day and the garden party.

VISITING ENTHUSIASTS

● Invite a new mother to visit, bring her baby and talk about all the things she has to do to help her baby grow.

● Invite adults who work with plants or animals to visit the group and show the children how to care for things that grow.

RESOURCE REQUESTS

● Ask parents to help the children find baby photographs of themselves and information about their first tooth, steps and words.

● Make a collection of baby clothes that the children have grown too big for.

● Ask parents to bring in flowerpots and safe garden tools for the garden centre role-play area.

THE GARDEN PARTY

● At the event, it may be helpful to have additional adult helpers to serve refreshments, play games and help children with the treasure hunt.

● Ask parents to grow seedlings and bring in plants from their gardens to sell at the garden party.

We have been using the theme of Growth to introduce your child to different areas of learning. If you would like to follow this up at home, here are a few ideas you might like to try.